Glad We

Written and Illustrated by Brad Tonner

ISBN: 1478397225
ISBN-13: 9781478397229

This book is dedicated to
Kelly and Jim.

All THE BEST
BRAD Tanner

Glad We Met

Written and Illustrated by Brad Tonner

Published by The Road Less Traveled Press

Once upon a time and just down the street
A wonderful red headed girl I happened to meet.

She was excited to find
an elephant lived right next door.
She told all her friends
"Could a girl ask for anything more?"

It was a friendship that some didn't think right.
But we knew right away it was love at first sight.
She had beautiful green eyes and lovely red hair.
Our friendship was magic,
which is something so rare.

We would celebrate anything just for pure fun.

Or we'd just relax and swing in
a hammock in the warm sun.

She'd hold my hand on the roller coaster,
to make me feel strong.

11

12

Or she'd make me feel at ease when others
thought our friendship was wrong.

She'd cook me fancy dinners and
make neat deserts with crunchies on top.
Or we'd laugh into the night
and never think we would stop.

15

We'd go out for a picnic
and look out at the sea.
She'd make me feel special
cause she'd just look at me.

I'd buy her presents for
no reason at all.
Just saying she liked it
made me feel 40 feet tall.

If she went to the doctors,
I'd hold her hand to make it all right.

Then she would snuggle with me
so I wouldn't feel lonely at night.

Sometimes we would sneak away
and spend a special day.

Or we would take a trip to a place far away.

We'd dress up in crazy costumes
for trick or treat.

Or we would go to a show and always
seem to get a front row seat.

We'd go to games and cheer
for our favorite teams.

We'd tell each other our secrets
and all our dreams.

She was someone who did everything right.
After all she was my princess and I was her knight.

One night we saw a star shoot across the sky.
We each made a special wish as it swooshed by.
She wished our friendship would
last year after year.
I told her that was my wish too,
so she had nothing to fear.

Like all fairy tales our friendship
will live long after we do.
It just has to be good and honest
and wonderful too.

Every fairy tale has a moral
words to live by.
They can be written in stone
or up in the sky.

Go out and live your life
and be who you want to be.
That will make you a success
in life and that's the key.

Then take that key and unlock every door.
You'll find a special someone
you'll never need more.

If your lucky you'll have a
wonderful friend for life.
Be it a special someone or a brother,
a sister a husband or a wife.

Never settle for second best
just to fit in.
That's the biggest mistake in life
and you'll never win.

If you're truly lucky like me you'll meet
a special someone right next door.
And you will live happily ever
after never asking for more.